is it okay to say this?

brief collected
notes, poems, and excerpts

trista mateer

Trigger warning for brief mention of sexual assault on pages 76 and 77.

ISBN: 9798825003184

Cover and interior design by Trista Mateer
Internal photos and art by Trista Mateer

For any inquiries please don't hesitate to get in touch.
tristamateerpoetry.com/contact
tristamateer@gmail.com
@tristamateer on TikTok and Instagram

For the parts of us we left behind.

is it okay
to say this?

You and I together
is the most foolish thing
I've ever hoped for.

You and I apart
is more foolish.

I know our love could wilt
out in the wild

but don't you think
we're made of sturdy stuff?

Don't you think
that we're enough?

Kiss me until nobody cares
about the metaphors anymore.

I am always moving toward you.

On my bad days, I say to myself: *then you.*
Sure, this now. But then you.

It's just my hard edges
and your hard edges
but I swear if we touch enough,
we'll be as smooth as skipping stones.

I'm a reader,
a compulsive book buyer,
a story hoarder.

I hate to admit it but I have to:

Hearing you talk about your day
for thirty minutes
sounds better than every book
I've saved from childhood
and tucked away on a shelf
for safe-keeping.

Cover to cover,
you're my favorite page turner.

is it okay to say this? - trista mateer

I want to get in an argument with your mouth
that neither of us can win,
tongues twisted up like roots.

I want to kiss you and feel like I am growing.

In this space right here
that we have made for each other,
you can say anything
and I will not abandon you.
Unwrap the worst things you have done.
Watch me hold them up to the light
and not even flinch.

what if our souls
are cosmically entwined?

what if i find you again
every time?

My love is a pair of scissors
I keep begging you not to run with.

I don't want either of us to get hurt.

I keep having dreams
of slicing into the globe
and carving out all of the places
you've kissed other people.

I could have had it easy
but I wanted it to hurt.
I wanted the unpragmatic love story.
I wanted to run across the world for someone.
I wanted the Earth to splinter.

September 19, 2020 at 3:05 AM

Fine I'll say it. I had the dream about you and the oranges again. I have written this poem at least four other times. I miss the thought of you in my bed. I can hold onto anything at night if I want it enough and I wanted it enough. I think you wanted it too. Inaction is the worst part of everything. I waited for you and I shouldn't have. I still love you just the same.

I know I've written too many poems about us

but poetry is the only proof I still have that any of this used to be worth holding onto.

You love me, yes.
But not in the way I deserve to be loved.

if you must shapeshift
to fit comfortably inside
your relationship

it is not worth it

please go

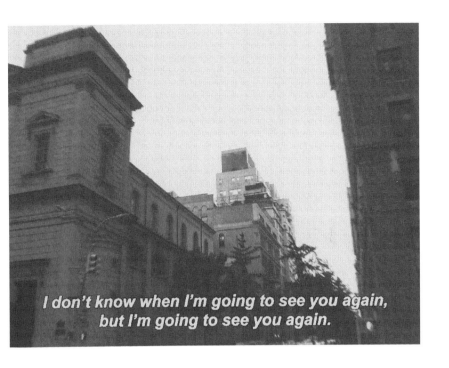

I don't know when I'm going to see you again,
but I'm going to see you again.

her cheeks bloom like roses,
but your garden has been empty
for a long time now
and it is not her job to fill it

Why am I so much better at missing you
than loving you?

Why I'm afraid this won't work:

You view love as a declaration.
I view love as an action.

Nothing feels right
when you're gone

but nothing feels right
when you're here
either.

I buzz like a fly around open mouths.

I want to get caught.
I want to find the sweet thing
        inside of everyone.
I want love to swallow me whole.

i still miss the sound
of your voice
singing off key

if you ever want to
i hope that you
call me

I loved a man who was afraid to look at himself in the mirror but had no problem looking at himself in my poetry.

Who could blame him?

I always wrote him better than he was.

is it okay to say this? - trista mateer

I STILL DON'T KNOW HOW TO MAKE A GRACEFUL EXIT

❮ Search   Done

April 23, 2016, 3:07 AM

So the boy you saved for later like an after dinner mint goes and gets himself married and you're left with nothing but spare change in your pocket it's not even enough for a bus ride home

people always talk about heartbreak
like it's localized pain
but it's not

it hurts everywhere

I know I deserve a love
that won't make me wait,
but I was so good
at waiting for you.

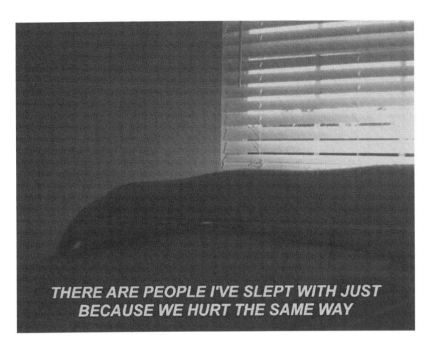

THERE ARE PEOPLE I'VE SLEPT WITH JUST
BECAUSE WE HURT THE SAME WAY

She does
not remind me
of anything.

Everything
reminds me
of her.

I miss the sound of your voice. Is it okay to say that? Is it also okay to say that I feel like I'm drowning? Both in overdramatic metaphors and in the absence of you?

I'm sorry for the poems.
All the shouting I did about your mouth.

You
were
the
tallest
tree
in
my
wild
heart.

Who would have thought I'd be the scissors?
I always wanted to be the lace.

Don't discount all the fires I fought
before you. I love you and all,
but you're a damn fool if you think
you could burn me up.

we're soulmates, you and I,
but that doesn't mean it works

that means my soul can't bear
to be without yours
but that doesn't mean it works

All my life I have been treated
like a match in the fingers of a child:
burnt out for pleasure
and dropped
at the slightest inconvenience.

You used to
make me feel safe
and you never will again.

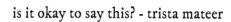

is it okay to say this? - trista mateer

oh no! it appears love is not going to save me from myself.

Sometimes I think
I resented you so much
it felt like love.

i can't stop thinking about you

My heart is a teenager with a ground floor bedroom and no screen in the window. It sneaks out at night. It comes and goes as it pleases. I'm at my wit's end trying to talk sense into it.

I don't know how our bodies

got so used to the space between them.

I stick to the ⬛⬛⬛ bad choice,
because it's full of ⬛⬛

you,

. And you. And you.

so her voice is the opposite of a lullaby / more like a moan in the dark / she is the thing that's been keeping me up nights.

in another life
we argue over
the grocery list
and your hips
are always in
close proximity
to my hips

I have written many versions of the same poem.
Always for you. Always for you.

My favorite story
is the one where you love me.

I tell it to myself so often
I forget it's mostly fiction.

In your anger and your despair
and your glorious, glorious youth:
do not discount the idea of soulmates.
Discount the idea of a singular soulmate.
You still have way too much to learn
to be taught by one person.

Write about what you need to write about even if it's just love poems. The world could always use at least six more love poems. And don't let anybody tell you otherwise.

hope

was telling
my mother
your name.

You used to hold all of my secrets.
Now you don't even want to hold
my name in your mouth.

I know everything that's ever
kept you up at night.

What am I supposed to do with that?

YOU ARE STILL
THE FIRST PERSON
I WANT TO SHARE
NEW THINGS WITH

Why did you leave?

It seemed healthier
than prodding a wound.
More sensible
than hurting in place.
I needed some air.

The first poem I wrote after you left
wasn't about love. For once
there were no lines to read between.
I didn't write your name
anywhere.

You wanted to know there was a place
love would always wait for you.

You wanted to go about your day
and come home to it
and sometimes not come home to it.

You wanted someone else
to do all the bleeding.

I know I have bigger problems
than who I'm not kissing right now
but three margaritas in,
I wonder how safe your number is
in my phone.

Grief is all I have left of you, so yes

I do hold onto it.

October 3, 2017 at 11:32 PM

Losing you

That's how I like to phrase it. Like you're just misplaced. Like I still might fight you somewhere.

is it okay to say this? - trista mateer

I keep shouting your name in the poetry
so I don't do it out loud.

Who has your back?
Who has your heart?
Who takes care of you?
Who takes you apart?

Don't you ever let
another human being
tear you apart.

Remember that you have
claws and teeth too.

Remember that you are
better off whole.

I keep seeing your writing on tumblr I think you're officially famous

When the boy who sexually assaulted me texts me politely to let me know he's been reading my poetry, my first instinct is to text him back.

I want to know which pieces he's read. If he tries to sort through the love poems looking for his. If he skips the ones about men who have hurt me. If his stomach ever churns at the details. I want to know if he remembers that July. I want to know if he sees himself reflected back in every poem about someone touching me with violence. If he can pick his hands out of the lineup. If he recognizes his own scent on the words.

I want to know if he'll keep reading when the poems get less ambiguous.

xxxxxxx xxxxxxx

You're lucky
the poems
don't have honest titles.

You never have to see
your name
next to what you did
with your hands.

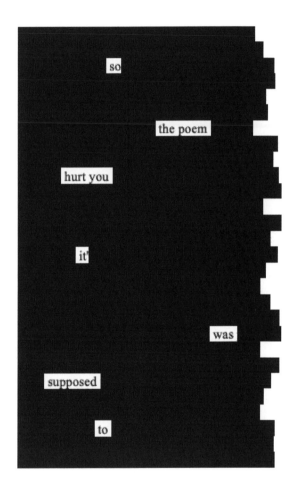

so

the poem

hurt you

it'

was

supposed

to

is it okay to say this? - trista mateer

when he was bored
he set fires in our bed

and had me crawl
over broken glass
to beg for the chance
to put them out

and I believed in love even when there was no reason to. even when I had to bleed for it. even when it stood me up. I happily spent most of my life waiting for it. to work out. to get better. to be worth it. I stayed long after I should have gone. I wish I could turn around and shake myself out of it. I wish I could reach through time just to tell her to run. in the middle of the night I whisper *go go go* and pray that she can hear it. years too late.

years too late.

Is it my job
as a woman,

to *encourage you*
to treat me like a person?

He'll help dig it but he won't
ever visit your grave.

Sure, that man wants you
but he hates you just the same.

‹ Search Done

March 1, 2021 at 8:13 PM

I GOT YOUR LETTER
I GUESS YOU KNEW BETTER
THAN TO PICK UP THE PHONE AND CALL
THANKS FOR SPARING ME YOUR VOICE
BUT I'D PREFER NOTHING AT ALL
I DON'T WANT APOLOGIES
SEEING YOU DOWN ON YOUR KNEES
DOES NOTHING
FOR ME ANYMORE

I don't miss you.

I miss the scenarios
I played out in my head at night
where you actually treated me
like I was a real person.

I'm Fine

is the kindest lie
I know how to tell.

If I'm honest
about how I'm feeling,

it might make people uncomfortable
but it also might keep me alive.

I miss you
       here

             and
             here

and

       here.
All the places
the line
    breaks.

When anything ends,
I tread water for thirty days.
I spend a month starving myself:
out of intimacy, out of love.
A month training myself
how to want from scratch,
how to exist without
someone else's hands on me.

God — it wasn't love.
It was just two people
barely surviving together.
One would have
smothered the other
for the promise
of a little light
in all that dark.

Change doesn't happen
overnight.

You are building a life
to be proud of.

A good and brave life.

That takes time.

The thing about love is that it ends more often than it doesn't. If you want to be a person who's good at love, you have to learn how to be a person who is good at handling endings. You have to accept that sometimes you're going to get walked away from and sometimes you're going to do the walking away and it is never going to be the end of the world for anyone.

grief grew like ivy
over your feet

you have been
standing in place
for too long

I like to tell myself that I wasn't
really in love with you but even on the months
I forget to pay my credit card bills,
I still remember to check your horoscope.

After the sting,

you have to give it a few minutes
but you're going to be fine.

Just hold on.
Have a seat.
Stay for a while.
Today, maybe tomorrow if you're up for it.
Reevaluate at a later date.
Part the curtains, open the blinds.
Not every day is going to feel like this one.
The quicksand of it.
The sinking.
Everything will shift if you give it time.
If you wait it out.
A little longer now.
A little longer.

If we both look at the same moon and you still don't want to call to say goodnight then maybe we're not looking at the same moon anymore.

Maybe the moon has nothing to do with it. Maybe you're not the same person.
Maybe I'm not.

you are standing
at the edge of a grave
shoveling dirt
over your own face

you can stop
any time now

Good things are happening.

I wish I could call
and tell you about them.

the fear and the prayer, alternatively

One day I will look back
at everything I wrote about you
and I will recognize the words
but not the feeling.

I've done
so much fucked up shit
just to try and let you go,
I'm afraid
that if I ever make it back
to California,
I won't be the same girl
you fell in love with.

Maybe that's okay.
Maybe I forgive you.
Maybe I don't.

i don't want to know
how you are,

but i always hope
things worked out
for you.

Surviving's ugly work
and here I am,
so hideously alive.

I still have a lot of growing to do and I know there is more room for it in your absence.

If you enjoyed this
collection, please consider
sharing it with a friend!

Also please know that
I deeply appreciate
when you take the time
to rate or review.

Thank you for your support!

Thank you for reading, always.

Tristan

APHRODITE MADE ME DO IT

poems, prose, and poetry

"IF YOU WERE ONLY MADE TO BE BEAUTIFUL, WE WOULDN'T HAVE PUT YOU DOWN HERE IN THE DIRT."

Part mythology retelling, part healing manifesto, this empowering and feminist collection tackles the timeless topic of love—romantic, platonic, and self-love—while also exploring various pieces of myth from Aphrodite's perspective.

OUT NOW

♡ ♡ ♡ ♡

ARTEMIS MADE ME DO IT

a reminder that you can't cage femininity

— MICHAELA ANGEMEER

I AM CALLING YOU HOME TO THE FOREST OF YOURSELF

Goddess of self-ownership. Portrait of women's rage. Artemis speaks to what is wild and untamed in all of us and in this collection she asks for a moment of calm.

OUT SEPTEMBER 6 2022
PREORDER NOW

more books by trista mateer

girl, isolated
A poignant portrait of mental health issues and creative burnout, written entirely between March 2020 and March 2021.

Honeybee
A collection of confessional sapphic poetry about coming out and also falling in and out of love with your best friend.

The Dogs I Have Kissed
Goodreads Choice for best poetry 2015. This collection tackles angry girlhood and intimacy issues.

Myth & Magick series
Aphrodite Made Me Do It
Artemis Made Me Do It
This series is a feminist exploration of Greek Mythology juxtaposed with poems about similar modern issues.

notes and credits

These lines, fragments, poems, and excerpts have been collected between 2013 and 2022. A few are from out of print books and chapbooks. Most were originally posted to Tumblr or Instagram. Some have been edited for clarity.

tristamateer.tumblr.com
instagram.com/tristamateer

excerpts from *The Dogs I Have Kissed*
pages 9, 12, 15, 75

excerpts from *Honeybee*
pages 47, 95, 98

excerpts from *girl, isolated*
pages 70, 105

TRISTA MATEER is a poet
and visual artist. Best
known for being sad
and sapphic online.

tristamateerpoetry.com
@tristamateer on instagram and tiktok